HOW TO ANALYZE PEOPLE

*The Complete Psychologist's Guide to Speed Reading
People – Analyze and Influence Anyone through Human
Behavior Psychology, Analysis of Body Language and
Personality Types*

Table of Contents

INTRODUCTION

Congratulations on getting a copy of *How to Analyze People: The Complete Psychologist's Guide to Speed Reading People – Analyze and Influence Anyone through Human Behavior Psychology, Analysis of Body Language and Personality Type.*

Body language can be likened to secret windows of the soul. Since our emotions are intertwined with our behavior, our inner feelings can appear through subtle body movements. Many of these slight changes are so innate, you may not even realize they are happening. Certain emotions like fear, lust, and euphoria can be detected through the manner in which a person moves the body. Many of these expressions are innate and are primal instincts. Much like a baby grasping the finger of his mother, he instinctively is communicating through movement.

One may conclude that understanding body language is a useless skill because we have the gift of verbal communication. While the art of linguistics is certainly necessary to communication, oftentimes, words only tell a small truth. People who lack the proper understanding of the connection between the body and mind will miss these slight signals. For example, the slight curve of the lips combined with a forward lean speaks attraction even if the words being spoken reveal the opposite. Imagine having the ability to detect when someone was lying by observing a simple eye movement.

There is a dynamic structure of the brain called the limbic system that is responsible for controlling how our emotions translate throughout our bodies. The limbic system controls our inner qualities such as the ability to nurture, express empathy, and even react to love. When your face suddenly blushes because you see your crush, that is your brain responding to the emotion of attraction. Without the limbic system, it would be increasingly difficult to be able to openly express our emotions through physical contact.

Animals Use Body Language to Communicate

Dogs are classic examples of animals who rely heavily on body movements to express themselves. Since they cannot verbalize their emotions to humans, they use their ears, paws, and even their tails to signal important symbols. Universally, a dog's tail wagging has been accepted as a dog showing his friendliness. However, not every wag is welcoming. A stiff, low wagging tail can indicate feelings of uneasiness. A straight, pointed wag is a sign of impending attack. Someone who generalizes all tail wagging as welcoming may encounter an unpleasant situation without the proper knowledge. Dog trainers initially begin their training with body movements to assign meanings to commands.

The same mentality rings true with humans. Many people may say one thing to appease the person they are around, yet their true intentions are masked. By understanding the psychology behind body language, you will be able to actually read people without them even knowing it. This ability comes in handy for the following situations:

- Raising a child

- Understanding your mate's true feelings

- Detecting lies or deception

- Spotting insecurity

- Emergency situations

Once mastered, you will be able to further develop your analytical skills and hone in on your ability to decode human behavior.

When raising young children, the ability to effectively communicate needs doesn't become apparent until around 15 months. Babies and toddlers rely heavily on certain nonverbal cues when communicating their needs. For example, children who experience inner conflict and lack the ability to express themselves verbally may bite their parents or peers as a means to seek attention.

This oral fixation is their way of getting their needs met. It is important for parents to understand the subtle movements of others in order to accurately meet the needs of their children.

Humans have used body language as a means of communication since the dawn of time. Before the traditional linguistic structure that we see today was developed, our ancestors relied heavily on innate body movements to express true emotions. In 1872, evolutionist Charles Darwin studied the behavior of humans and animals in his book, *The Expression of the Emotions in Man and Animals*. He analyzed carefully how animals communicate non-verbally and made scientific comparisons to humans. Without his groundbreaking revelations, different forms of education like anthropology, social sciences, and even kinesics would be irrelevant. As more psychological evidence has appeared, thus proving the existence of legitimate body cues, we have the ability to assign meanings to intricate expressions.

There are plenty of books on this subject on the market. Thanks again for choosing this one, please enjoy!

CHAPTER 1

MASTERING THE ART OF ANALYZING PEOPLE - BODY LANGUAGE 101

Body Language Clues: The Basics

When individuals communicate, the face is typically the focal point. The lips are home to revealing contextual clues towards a person's thoughts. For example, when the lips begin to draw inward towards the mouth, a person may be hiding something. They may have a secret or detail they want to share with you, but are apprehensive due to various reasons. This is sometimes known as "lip swallowing" as a person is physically stopping themselves from revealing what they truly want to say.

Many attribute a sad face with the corners of the lips pointing downward. Some individuals rest their lips in this position on a regular basis. This could indicate an inward turmoil or grief they are experiencing. Many of us encounter melancholy individuals whether personally or in the workplace. The next time you are speaking to them, pay attention to the positioning of their lips. You may have a solid backing for viewing them as being generally sad.

People who frequently bite their lips may deal with chronic anxiety or are showing you that they are uncomfortable. Many times, an unpleasant conversation, stress, or nervousness will show through biting. This action is almost like a safe space for individuals as it provides them with comfort in the midst of anxiety.

Signs Given Through the Nose

Although commonly ignored, the nose can signal various emotions such as aggression, displeasure, and even brainstorming. When people are deep in thought, you may notice that they tend to play with the tip of their nose by wiggling or even making an imprint on it. A slight pinch shows frustration; perhaps a person cannot figure out a solution.

You have likely heard the reaction of a person being provoked. However, the nose can signal the true nature of their next move. When the nostrils flare, a person is experiencing a great deal of adrenaline due to feelings of extreme anger. They may be reaching their limit in an argument and gearing themselves up for the next level. When you notice this, perhaps de-escalate the conversation until that person can calm down. They may be using this intense form of breathing as ammunition to explode!

What Your Eyebrows Are Saying

The forehead works in conjunction with the eyes and eyebrows to signal astonishment with slight wonder. Maybe you are retelling an exciting story, and the person doesn't quite believe the extremity of it. Their forehead may wrinkle to indicate disbelief. This doesn't mean they think you are a liar. Rather, they are surprised by the story's context which makes them want to know more.

The eyebrows are just as expressive as the eyes themselves. Since they are flexible to a certain degree, they are able to be animated. As mentioned, a wrinkled forehead can be associated with shock. Often, this is accompanied by raised eyebrows. This positioning of the face is aligned with the common "gasp" expression used in illustrations.

When lowered, the brows can signal a plethora of emotions from confusion to irritation. Speculation is the commonality between the different signals given off by the brows. In addition, a lowered brow could indicate disrespect. In an argument, oftentimes, one misspoken phrase can set off a round of lowered brows followed by the head slanting backwards.

Cartoons may depict a hunky man raising and lowering his eyebrows up and down when looking at an attractive woman. These actions are often expressed in an extreme manner. Although entertaining, illustrators are correct with their depiction. Brows moving in a quick up and down motion can signify recognition.

When we run into an old friend at a crowded coffee shop, our eyebrows may quickly jolt up and down.

These are examples of subtle movements taking place in unlikely areas of the face. The eyes were purposely left out as we will dive deeper into their meaning later. Although the face is home to distinct signs of emotion, the body can radiate similar clues to indicate feelings.

Body Cues

When engaging in a conversation, leaning in towards your partner reveals interest. While eating dinner, a woman may lean in towards her date with her entire body pointed in his direction. When this occurs, all areas of the body are facing the subject at hand. Even the fingers, toes, knees, and nose are facing the opposite person. In many instances, legs leaning towards a love interest while sitting could indicate a desire for a sexual encounter.

A hunched back with shoulders pointing inward indicates anxiety or sadness. When the body curls inward, this demonstrates fear. Your body is trying to protect itself instinctively. When a child is embarrassed, you will often notice their head, shoulders, and arms dropping in an obvious manner. In adults, we are conditioned to hide emotions such as embarrassment, anxiety, or fear. Because of this, the signs are subtle. At the root of all emotions such as embarrassment, anxiety, or sadness is fear. Fear of the unknown, fear of what others are thinking, and fear of the future. With the body curling inward, you may suddenly feel safe and less vulnerable. To prove this, imagine a time where you were embarrassed by a mistake at work. Perhaps your boss confronted you about it in a less than ideal manner. Did you have to force your body to stand tall to exude confidence? If so, you probably had to work at holding yourself upright.

The chest is a silent means of flirtation for both men and women. Men may point their chest outward to show masculinity. A woman may entice by pointing her chest towards her interest in order to expose her breasts. In addition, women may slightly turn their chest to about 45 degrees in order to further pronounce their figure.

A chest that is curving inward is a protective mechanism. Animals, as mentioned in the outset, have a similar body language that communicates dominance or submission. When a wolf is showing his alpha that he is not a threat, he will curve his chest inward, thus concealing his strength. This isn't an inviting pose, but rather, a sign that he isn't seeking conflict. Humans display these same tendencies. A successful CEO may relax the chest and position it inward when wanting to appear humble towards employees. This pose, although it translates insecurity, can be a friendly, submissive gesture, perhaps even signaling respect.

Signs of the Shoulders, Neck, and Hips

In a similar fashion, when the shoulders, neck, and back are upright, this person is demonstrating confidence. However, the need for authoritative power could shift the shoulders from an upright positioning to one that looms over as a means to show intimidation. Notice how the shoulders, even though being portrayed as upright, still slightly curl. Although this person is clearly trying to establish authority, there is still a slight insecurity or protection in his stance. This is a key sign in revealing people who may appear confident, but are truly insecure about something deep down.

The back is powerful and direct. When you are conversing with someone, and they keep their back turned away from you, likely, they are not interested in what you have to say. In addition, this could be another sign of attempting to give off dominance. This dismissive behavior is condescending to the person they are engaging with and makes them less approachable.

The hips make subtle movements but powerful demands. Generally, the hips are used with sexual communication, thus inviting or rejecting a potential partner. When pushed outward or swayed, the invitation for flirtation is abundant. A person may show their attraction in this manner. Similarly, the direction that the hips are pointing towards could also signal the direction that person wants to go.

Body language is a beautiful tool that allows truth to emanate. Body language is all about association. The directions that we typically link to emotions can reveal the true state of a person. In order to effectively master this language, it's important to understand basic psychological principles. When assigning deeper meaning to common motion, you are thinking like a psychologist. As mentioned, the previous examples only scratch the surface to what the body is telling us. As we dive into the complexities of body language, you will see how intricate and detailed this communication form truly is.

CHAPTER 2

UNDERSTANDING THE SELF - WHAT DOES MY BEHAVIOR DISPLAY?

In order to properly analyze others, it is important to seek understanding with your own body movements. In social settings, the way we position our body can be the difference between making friends and repelling them. Since we cannot see our body movements as well as others, it's important to become in tune with your feelings and perception. Many times, we may not even realize the silent signals we are giving off. Sure, we have the ability to speak our emotions, but we all know that the truth is seldom spoken.

Science has proven that we emit energy that can be detected, and is even contagious. When your inner energy is feeling tired or bored, your outward appearance will give evidence of that energy despite how "excited" you say you are. Technology has given us the grand opportunity to display rejection with the simple glance down at the phone. For example, when a friend is telling you a story that you are 100 percent not interested in, likely you will reach for your phone and begin scrolling. Your words are saying, "Uh-huh," occasionally, but your demeanor speaks volumes. You may believe you are listening when really you are showing outward disdain for your friend. This sign is often taken as disrespect and could create distance in the friendship.

Another common sign is the crossing of the arms. In social occasions, this can be translated as, "I don't want to be here." When in reality, you could simply be cold. Since this is what you are exhibiting, others are naturally going to view you as unapproachable. Do you find yourself doing this quite often? Crossing of the arms is another form of protection. It is almost likened to a comfort mechanism that we do when in an uncomfortable situation.

This can be attributed to a form of social anxiety and inner insecurity. Sure, you may be the most inviting person in the room, but you are not aware of that yet. Your inner, primal voice is activating your fight or flight response. You may be subconsciously uncomfortable with your outfit, afraid of others' opinions, or even fearful of talking to people. The importance of becoming aware of your deeper desires will work wonders towards your body language.

Another instance occurs during one-on-one communication. Do you notice your eyes drifting during a conversation? Or even your hand being placed on your face while someone is talking? This signals disinterest and could be extremely disrespectful to the person talking. In turn, your friend could become upset with you without you even realizing it.

Flirtation can be a fine and tricky art because many of the signals of genuine interest and attraction are often intertwined. For example, a young man was engaging in a conversation with a married woman at a public event. She was talking to him about a job opportunity she had available in her department. Being recently laid off from his job, naturally, the man was excited! He began to shift his body towards her as he leaned his head in. His eyes never left hers, and he had a slight smile on his face. Upon noticing, the woman's husband grew increasingly alert to their conversation. From the outside, all he saw was this young man, leaning in towards his wife with a smile. Unbeknownst to him, the situation was far from flirtatious.

This is a clear indicator of how our body language deeply affects the way people view us. When engaging in that conversation, the young man was extremely interested in the possible job opportunity, not the married woman. However, his body language signaled attraction. The importance of being aware of how your body is positioned when speaking to others is a subliminal sign of respect. One fantastic way to become aware of your body motions is to remember the three W's: who, what, and where. Let's consider them one at a time.

Who

When speaking with another person, it's key to remember who you are engaging with. Is it a close friend of the opposite sex? Is it your manager or maybe even an older person? In all of these instances, the way you position your body means everything. Take, for example, speaking with your manager. Do you find yourself naturally crossing your arms when he or she approaches you? This could be your way of protecting yourself against their authority, or you may actually dislike your manager. However, you want to keep your job and even appear interested in what he or she has to say. This instance is when acting and awareness play a major role.

When you see your manager coming, the butterflies may ensue. You may even become a bit clammy in the hands. Instead of allowing that feeling to overpower you, simply acknowledge it, and let it be. Don't try to manipulate the feeling as that causes further anxiety. Rather, acknowledge it, and place your hands by your side with open palms. Try your best to breathe and remain comfortable. Position your back upright with your shoulders aligned. Create an opening demeanor that opens the door for conversation.

What

When engaging in a conversation, try to feel what your body is doing. Are your hands clenched in a fist? Do you feel your face tightening as if you're displeased? When you become aware of what your body does when engaging in a conversation, you will be able to control those muscles. One vital question you can ask yourself is,

"What is my body telling others right now?" By doing so, you can immediately change the way others perceive you.

Where

It's especially important to be cognizant of where you are when speaking to others. Oftentimes, certain atmospheres may warrant specific behavior. For example, during a blind date, it would be quite rude to scrunch your forehead and brows in disgust at your date's appearance. Sure, they may not be what you expected, but you never want to display your inner emotions. In addition, you wouldn't walk into a funeral with a big smile and open arms. Even if you barely knew the deceased, that demeanor may appear heartless to the grieving family. Making the connection between what your body is doing and remembering where you are is imperative for your reputation.

Body awareness is key to navigating your world. It is defined as "the sense that we have of our own bodies." It is an understanding of the parts that make up one's body, where they are located, how they feel, and even what they can do. Certain activities such as yoga and Pilates assist with connecting the bridge between the body and mind. When engaging in these exercises, you are mentally aware of the positioning of your body. You have full control over your balance which strengthens your mental and physical muscles. Engaging in these activities on a regular basis can assist with understanding your body movements. This will come in handy when evaluating what your body is doing in social settings.

To practice your own proprioception exercise at home, begin by balancing on one foot. What are your arms doing? Your fingers? Do you feel a tingle in your opposing leg? Become engrossed in how your body is working together to keep you balanced. By repeating this simple exercise daily, you'll begin to notice the movements of even the smallest parts of your body.

In order to fully understand the body language of others, you have to become connected with your personal movements. Body language is more than just reading movements. It's attributing a deeper meaning towards body posture that can speak volumes into a person's emotions.

CHAPTER 3

IT'S ALL IN THE EYES - CLUES TO REVEALING TRUE INTENTIONS

When children are being evaluated for neurological challenges, one of the main observable points is their ability to maintain good eye contact. Although an intricate detail, the ability to lock eyes with someone else during conversation speaks wonders to the child's level of function. If a child is able to maintain direct eye contact throughout the course of their assessments, they are deemed high on the social spectrum. However, the inability to maintain eye contact could be a sign of autism or even social anxiety. The eyes reveal small truths to the inner workings of our biology.

Typically, what is the first thing you look at when meeting someone? Usually, their eyes reveal aspects of beauty that are attractive to first encounters. Many even remember people because of the shape, color, and size of the eyes. We are neurotically programmed to be visual creatures who make associations through what we see. Generally, these associations are labeled by what we give off. Since every aspect of the body works in conjunction with the brain, how do our eyes communicate with certain receptors?

The Eye Meets the Brain

The retina is like the gatekeeper of the eye. Everything we see, through the exchange of light, passes through the retina and is then transferred to two different aspects of the eye: rods which manage our ability to see at night, and cones which handle our daily vision activities such as color translation, reading, writing, and scanning. Various neurons travel throughout the eye and communicate with different functions within the eye to carry unique signals. These signals are then carried through the optic nerve into the cerebral cortex. The cerebral cortex is like the movie theatre of the brain. It controls our visual receptors that are responsible for perception, memory, and thoughts. When our eye sees something pleasurable, researchers have discovered that the pupil actually expands. This phenomenon proves that what we see is how we think. Through this, we can formulate opinions, draw conclusions, and even interpret body movements.

There are certain concrete directions carried out by the eyes that indicate true intentions:

Right glance: This is used to remember something, maybe a name, face, song, or book.

Left glance: This is used to remember physical features such as color, shape, texture, and other visual stimulants.

Glancing downward in a right position: This controls our imagination and what we believe something to be like.

Glancing downward towards the left: Inner communication, the conversations we have with the self.

The way our eyes work with the brain and perception is key to understanding body language. Since we use every aspect of our body to communicate, it is only natural that the eyes play a major role in this form of communication. Sure, the eyes may seem one dimensional to the untrained individual. However, their slight movements can indicate everything you need to know about a person. Let's consider a few examples.

Direct Eye Contact

Direct eye contact can mean a caveat of emotions. Surely, self-confidence is one of the primary indicators of locking eyes. When vetting for a job, recruiters will often instruct their interviewees to look the interviewer in the eye in order to display awareness. This shows the interviewer that you aren't intimidated and can take on any task. Similarly, animals utilize eye contact when interpreting dominance. For example, a trainer will often look a dog in the eye that he is training in order to establish dominance. By the trainer locking eyes and refusing to move, the dog will know to listen to his commands. Humans also communicate via dominant signals.

Direct eye contact trumps fear. It shows that you are comfortable with the conversation, and it even indicates interest.

In addition, balance is the key to everything. Too much direct eye contact could prove to be intimidating to the receiving individual. This intense stare could cause others to feel uncomfortable, with them maybe even questioning your overall sanity. Imagine engaging in a conversation with someone who never stopped looking into your eyes. Even when you looked away, their eyes were still locked on yours. Surely, you would chalk them up to be extremely strange. It's always important to be cognizant of what your eyes are doing as staring, in some cultures, could be viewed as rude.

Looking Away

When a person avoids eye contact, this is typically a sign of low self-confidence. The person may be uncomfortable with the conversation, person, or environment they are in. In addition, anxiety surrounding social settings can make a person apprehensive to locking eyes with someone they don't know. Avoiding eye contact also signals inner conflict. Perhaps they are fighting against subconscious urges of attraction; therefore, they avoid making eye contact; or maybe they are hiding something that heightens their anxiety. This doesn't indicate that a person is devious or even untrustworthy. They may suffer from debilitating self-consciousness that overwhelms their disposition.

Dilated Pupils

The pupils generate intricate signals that identify even the smallest of changes within the body. Studies have shown that when people are presented with a challenging question, their pupils grow larger. When the brain is forced to think beyond its capabilities, the pupils actually become narrow, according to a 1973 study. The pupils are also key indicators of stress on the brain. Health care professionals will shine a small flashlight into the eyes of their patients in order to check the normality of their pupils. If the pupils are balanced in size and react to the shining light, the brain isn't experiencing distress. However, any imbalance could indicate a serious brain injury.

As mentioned earlier, dilated pupils express extreme interest, even agreement. When you see or hear something that sparks your attention, your pupils will dilate almost immediately. The same occurs when a person is shown a representation of something they agree with. In 1969, a revered researcher sought to prove the notion that the pupils' dilation can reveal political affiliations. By showing participants pictures of political figures they admired, the participants' eyes dilated. However, when shown an opposing photo, the pupils grew narrow; often snake-like.

What Our Visual Directions Indicate

The positioning of our eyes and what we choose to focus on during a conversation can speak volumes. For instance, glancing downward could indicate shame, even submission. When children are being reprimanded, they are often looking down to show their personal disdain for their behavior. In ancient Chinese culture, one typically looked down in a submissive form to show respect to those in authority. On the contrary, glaring upward indicated traits of haughtiness. It is often associated with being bored or not wanting to engage in the activity at hand. In addition, looking up signals uncertainty. Movies and television shows may depict a teenager taking a test and looking up because they are unaware of the answer.

Sideways glances are often cues for internal irritation. For example, when a co-worker you dislike walks into the room, you may inadvertently look at them sideways, simply because they are the bane of your existence. This can also occur when engaging with individuals who annoy you. The takeaway from the sideways stare is discontentment. When you see something that just isn't right, or even a sneaky individual, you may give them the side-eye. This demonstrates total repulsion for their attitude, reputation, or even their expressions.

Many would attribute squinting to being unable to see. While true, a squint can also mimic signs of disbelief or confusion. One may hear something and want more information. Thus, they squint their eyes while listening; it's almost as if they are saying, "I don't believe you...I need more answers!"

Stress can induce quick blinking which causes a person to go into a frenzy. You may notice a person rapidly blinking while moving frantically to finish a task. This could be accompanied by sweat or trembling. On the contrary, excessive blinking could be a subtle sign of arrogance. A boss, for example, may blink rapidly while speaking to an employee in an attempt to dismiss their conversation. This fast-action blinking essentially blinds the boss from the employee for less than a second, indicating that they would rather be engaging in something else.

A direct gaze paired with a lowered lid and head indicates extreme attraction. It's almost likened to a "come hither" invitation between mates. This gaze is heightened through sexual attraction and may even induce pupil dilation.

Inability to Focus and Attention Deficit

An eye nystagmus identifies how long it takes the body to focus on one point after undergoing extreme movement. If a person has a nystagmus lasting longer than 14 seconds, they may have challenges with keeping focused. One academic facility tests the accuracy of a child's nystagmus by spinning them a number of times and having them glance up towards the ceiling. The eyes then move rapidly, sometimes dilating, then narrowing. The longer it takes the child to stabilize is documented. They further engage in this spinning activity weekly with the hopes of strengthening their ability to remain focused on one thing despite many distractions. As they continue to grow a tolerance, their eyes will stabilize in a lower amount of time. The goal is to strengthen their ability to dismiss outward distractions which will help with attention deficit disorder. The movement of the eyes tell trained professionals exactly how much assistance a child will need and in what specific area. Aren't the eyes magnificent?

Our eyes open the door to many revelations of the self. You are able to gain psychological perspective on how you perceive yourself and others by a simple glance! Irritation, lust, attraction, and even doubt can be detected by paying close attention. Since the eyes have a direct pathway to the brain, it is only natural that they are the gatekeepers of the soul. By implementing these quick tips into your social life, you will have the grand ability to analyze a person in a complex manner. Of course, the eyes are also home to detecting deceit. As we continue to travel through our body language adventure, we will soon learn how the eyes can reveal the trustworthiness of an individual.

CHAPTER 4

THE CUES THAT TELL IT ALL - CONTEXT TRUMPS WORDS

Universally, there are certain facial expressions that demolish all cultural divides. Researchers conclude that all over the world, happiness, sadness, surprise, fear, disgust, and anger are all expressed in the same manner. Gesturing, as well as touching, gives off certain signals that assist with emotions.

However, nonverbal communication essentially means reading between the lines and seeking truth in the midst of words. A person may be saying one thing, but their tone means another. Researchers have grouped nonverbal communication into five categories. Let's consider them each.

1. Repetition

When engaging in a conversation, it is useful to repeat what the other person has said so as to improve memory. When a person verbally repeats what you said to them, they are demonstrating that your statement matters. They want to be able to access that information at a later time. In addition, this may be used as a signal that they are listening to what you're saying. Be careful, though, as too much repetition could be an irritation to some. They may misunderstand your listening cues as condescending as this is what mothers do to children when they learn to speak.

2. Contradiction

Contradiction is one of the more obvious cues that signal disapproval. Often times, these subtle contradictions could be used to demean another or express dominance. One of the primary examples of this occurs in the workplace. For example, a controlling manager overhears her employee speaking with a customer. The customer is asking about a specific protocol. The employee is attempting to describe an easier way to accomplish her goal. Upon hearing, the manager immediately steps in, tells the employee that her way is incorrect and proceeds to direct the customer herself. Imagine how that employee feels. Not only was she embarrassed in front of a client, but her notability was questioned. This contradiction caused the customer to view the employee as someone who isn't well-versed. The manager could have handled the situation in a more graceful manner, and likely, this was done out of an attempt to prove dominance.

3. Substitutions

Do you remember that look your mother gave you when she meant what she said? Likely, you can envision those stern eyes, scrunched mouth, and serious demeanor. Your mother didn't have to utter one phrase for you to understand that your current behavior was unacceptable. Daily, we use substitutions as a means to communicate. These intense glares or slight glances can speak volumes to people who know each other well. They may also indicate emphasis on a certain command. Dogs operate primarily through vocal substitutions. When you loom over a dog while stating, "Back," they know that area is off limits to them. The actual word is being substituted for an understandable action.

4. Complimenting

When a young man performs well at his baseball game, onlookers can see the coach patting him on the back or even giving him a high five. These outward displays of approval are well-known cues that signify a job well done. We may give a wink, hand gesture, or even a hug to express proud emotions towards others. This mild stamp of approval crosses masculine and feminine roles as well. Football players are often seen patting the butts of their teammates to signify a job well done. When conducted between romantic interests, this could be an outward sexual invitation.

5. Accenting

This occurs when people want their voices to be heard. They may slam their bedroom doors after yelling a remark, or clap their hands to express seriousness. This can be likened to accenting a specific word. That small dash brings emphasis to one or more of the noted letters. Thus, it alerts the reader to change their pronunciation. Similarly, accenting in nonverbal cues could signal a change of behavior. When analyzing individuals with deep-rooted insecurities, they may rely heavily on accenting their words in order to appear dominant. They are hoping to ignite fear in their subjects as a means of control.

Gestures can accentuate a conversation and create excitement. Typically, individuals who utilize gestures are described as, "people who talk with their hands." These movements can emphasize the plot of a story or even bring light to a discourse. They are descriptive in nature, and are used to keeping the attention of an audience or an individual. Public speaking classes place a great deal of weight on the importance of using gestures in their delivery. They bring warmth to the words being spoken in addition to liveliness.

One of the primary ways to build a human connection is through touch. The embracing touch coming from a friend or a stranger can alleviate stress and create a sense of community. When grieving, oftentimes, words from well-intended individuals are not enough. However, a soft touch of the hand speaks, "I am here for you," in a way that words could never express. The reason being is that touching is an action. You are physically showing someone your interest in them. In addition, touching hands can signify a person's personality. Certain managers judge potential candidates based upon their handshake. If they encounter a weak shake, the boss can pick up on their timid nature. They may shy away from hiring them in a fast-paced environment. On the other hand, a firm shake exudes confidence. The hiring manager may consider that candidate because they didn't display fear.

Across various cultures, the amount of personal space given is varied. East Asian cultures typically stand about one to two inches away from the person they are engaging with. This displays a sign of respect and interest. In the United States, however, we may view that spatial closeness as intruding. We may even feel uncomfortable as to what the person's intentions are. However, creating too much space could trigger your householder into thinking you don't want to be around them. Creating a balanced view of spatial awareness is important to communicating effectively. Take a look at the distance between the tip of your pointer finger and your inner elbow. This is the proper amount of allotted space that will allow you to converse comfortably with your partner.

The manner in which someone speaks can also indicate personality traits. Usually, grade school teachers will speak to their students in a high-pitched voice, as it ignites excitement and is inviting. However, that level of excitement may not be warranted at an all-adult function. In fact, if they tried to speak to another adult in that manner, the receiving adult may take it as the person being condescending. It is useful to consider the tone in which you are speaking so as not to come off as being rude, sarcastic, or even flirty. Creating a balanced manner of speaking while interjecting inflections when necessary will help you to effectively communicate without offense.

Nonverbal communication can be acquired through analyzing simple cues that occur daily. You may ask yourself, "When someone speaks to me in this way, how do I feel?" or, "Am I comfortable when someone else is this close to me?" By asking yourself these simple questions, you will be able to effectively communicate with others while picking up on their cues.

CHAPTER 5

ESSENTIAL TOOLS THAT GIVE YOU AN EDGE ANALYZING BEHAVIOR

The next section will get into the "bread and butter" of our discussion. Body language is an entire psychology that assigns significant reasons behind behavior. Understanding these reasons will give you dominance over others because it emphasizes humanity. You are taking the additional time to become educated on understanding someone else. This places great emphasis on empathy as it forces you to become connected with another human. Imagine being able to understand the context of what someone else is saying as opposed to taking their words literally. You will likely be able to communicate effectively and make strategic moves. You will no longer obsess over small intricacies as you will already have the definitive answer. As you read, imagine someone in your life who displays the qualities presented. How have you previously engaged with them? Has your experience been positive or negative? Have your misunderstandings sparked the need to resolve conflict or ignite it? When you learn how to "work the system," so to speak, you will gain insight into how to effectively break the barriers of communication and emphasize understanding. These tools are imperative to your reputation, social success, and even productivity. When seeking to gain a better understanding of the behavior of others, it's wise to consider these three aspects:

1. Can I separate my previous preconceived notions from what is occurring in front of me?

2. Can I somehow make a valuable difference in this person's life by picking up on their social cues?

3. Am I willing to confront situations of deceit or attraction head on so as to fulfill my personal needs?

4. The ability to read the language of others comes with a weighty responsibility. You are essentially able to decode truth. You must then develop a proper way to confront certain revelations head on. This is where building your ability to effectively communicate comes into play. By learning how to state your opinion without embarrassing the other person, you can use your new talent for the betterment of society.

CHAPTER 6

HOW TO INTERPRET VERBAL COMMUNICATION

A young student has worked over 20 hours to complete a 40-page essay for her college class. She then had to develop a visual representation to accompany her presentation. After three restless nights and countless cups of coffee, she is finally ready to present her finished report to the class. After performing an engaging and educational discourse, she breathed a deep sigh of relief. After class, she approached her professor and asked him how he enjoyed it. Barely looking up from his computer, the professor stopped and said, "It was fine," in a monotone voice. She was devastated. After dedicating all of her time and resources to this project, she was not satisfied with, "It was fine." A week later, after wondering what she could have improved upon, she finally got her grade back. Shaking, she opened the link and saw a 100% grade. She was ecstatic. She felt greatly accomplished and proud of her work. However, she still wondered why the professor gave her that response if he was going to give her an A.

The professor could have genuinely loved her presentation. In fact, it could have given him chills. However, because he was so monotone in his response, the student grew insecure. He gave off the impression that he did not appreciate all of her hard work. In reality, the professor greatly enjoyed it; so much so, he gave her a perfect grade. What is the issue with his actions?

Likely, you would conclude that the way he uttered, "It was fine," was a turn off. That monotone delivery is quite different from the excited, "It was fine!" paired with a clap. This is the power of verbal communication. Although one person may say one thing, the way they speak it reveals the truth. Our body language works closely with the manner in which we speak. A rather rude comment can be overlooked when paired with a smiling face, or it could be taken as extremely creepy. In addition, a smile can hide insidious intentions. This is why body language is a compilation of various components.

When a person constantly speaks in a harsh, assertive, and bold manner, others may conclude that that person is angry. They may even avoid associating with them for fear of embracing negative energy. In reality, the person could be amicable and positive. However, the way they place great emphasis on certain words or topics is intimidating. The power of tone, emphasis, and volume can create great conclusions when it comes to reputation. However, there are exceptions to this theory. Some individuals may express themselves one way, yet their actual personality is quite different. Take, for example, the late Michael Jackson. Michael had an extremely light and timid voice. He would speak almost like an unsure child, retelling a bedtime story. Upon only hearing him, one may conclude that Michael was submissive, shy, and quiet. The reality of his persona was quite different. The innovation found within his music and the creativity exuded through his dance moves illuminated great power and confidence. Despite the volume, tone, and inflection of his voice, he was a mighty lion when it came to his craft. Personal friends and family members, however, knew that somewhere, deep inside, lived a submissive, shy, and quiet person. This denotes that within our voice, despite intention, lie deep-rooted personality traits that we may be blind to. The loud and boisterous individual may be seeking to compensate for a deep insecurity. The arrogant and assertive lawyer may be fuming with angry emotions. The way in which a person speaks is complex and reveals truth.

The power behind how you say something can turn your innovative idea into a passed opportunity. Imagine pitching an idea for a new innovation with a monotone voice and no sign of excitement. Surely, those on the other end would not be convinced this is your passion. You may have missed your opportunity simple because you lacked enthusiasm. Your voice can also be a manipulative tool used to assert to others. There is a stark distinction between yelling rules and explaining them. The way a person says something can make a difference in how the sentence is perceived. A stressed manager can assert, "Why are you always late?" to an employee with a stern voice and a frowning mouth. Or she could kindly say, "Why are you always late?" with a slight touch on the shoulder and a concerned tone. This could be the moment where the employee either opens up or seeks further employment. When you think about it, words are just extensions of the mind. We all use them and express ourselves in one way or the other. However, the tone can drastically alter our perceived intentions and even our reputation.

The volume in which one speaks can ignite action. A whisper may indicate confidential information, while a loud yelp could signal, "Get away." In addition, a monotone voice could indicate disinterest where an emphasis on words and syllables could signal excitement. Sarcasm, on the other hand, is quite tricky to decode as it is subjective to the person speaking. One lively individual could show sarcasm in the same manner they would offer a greeting. This is where contextual clues come into play. Analyze the person's body language. Do they have a slight smile or a straight face? Does what they say seem outlandish in relation to the topic at hand? Interpreting sarcasm involves integrative techniques to understanding. It is a complex system that is unique to each person. One of the primary reasons why sarcasm is so difficult to understand for some is because it can mimic traditional body language cues. In this respect, it may be essential to get to know the person you are speaking with, so they can better understand your personality. Then, little by little, bring on the sarcasm!

Understanding your personal inflection can affect your reputation. You may have the purest of intentions, but your diction, volume, and choice of words is taken adversely. Others may create a distance between themselves and you due to this inconsistency. Being cognizant of the way you say something can be a true indicator of your intention. In addition, your communication skills will operate smoothly. The two main components of mastering effective communication are control and awareness. It is important to control the tone, inflection, and volume of your voice. It may even be necessary to control the type of words you use. Next, being aware of your audience, surroundings, and mood can play a huge role in how your words come off. A bad or melancholy mood may not be suitable for a children's book reading at the library. You can practice altering your verbal skills by seeking feedback from others. Have them analyze how you express a sentence, and they can provide constructive ways to improve.

CHAPTER 7

DESTROY PERCEPTION AND BUILD UNDERSTANDING

Unfortunately, many missed opportunities, acts of violence, and lapses of judgment occur due to inaccurate perception. Many people lose the opportunity to connect with others because they rely so heavily on initial judgment. Perception is defined as, "the ability to see, hear, or become aware of something through the senses." We gather conclusions about people from the information we receive from them. If we have a negative encounter, likely, we will perceive that person in a bad light. Body language and perception are the two components that equal a conclusion. The way someone positions themselves, holds their hands, or even moves their eyes can be taken a certain way. Although perceiving body language is a natural part of social development, perception can always be altered. We have the grand ability to be able to acknowledge something without jumping to conclusions. Is this really possible when interpreting body language?

Absolutely! One of the primary keys to building understanding is letting go of preconceived associations. For example, a young woman is always standing with her hands crossed, eyes lowered, and mouth downturned. Upon looking at her, you could conclude that she is prudish, stuck up, and distant. This may prevent you from speaking to her. In reality, the young woman is far from stuck up. Rather, she suffers from social anxiety and is uncomfortable in large crowds. She has a fear of carrying on a conversation along with personal insecurities. She desperately wants to make friends but doesn't want to make the first move. This disconnect creates a whirlwind of false notions that prevents pure human connection. Since one person perceives her as being stuck up, they avoid sparking a conversation without truly getting to know her personality. This occurs often and is the result of misunderstandings.

Breaking down those preconceived notions about certain behavior involves eliminating one-way thinking. As opposed to assigning only one meaning to a specific body movement, open your mind to the possibility of other reasonings behind behavior. Environmental factors may even alter traditional body language meanings. Crossed arms usually translate to feelings of self-consciousness or disapproval. However, in an extremely cold room, does it have the same meaning? When talking with a friend during a sunny day, does their looking to the side mean they are lying? Or could the sun be extraordinarily bright? Situational factors are also imperative to drawing definite conclusions. Breaking eye contact doesn't automatically mean your friend isn't interested in your conversation. Perhaps they are fatigued or swamped with personal issues at the moment. It's important to be flexible with how you perceive behavior. By understanding that there is always a reason behind everything, you will learn to give others the benefit of the doubt.

The traditional saying, "You can't judge a book by its cover," is vital to making social connections. A woman with scrunched brows, a downturned mouth, and hooded eyes may give off the impression that she is always angry. However, upon getting to know her, you realize she is extremely friendly. Perhaps that is the natural structure of her face. The same rings true for a man who engages in deep eye contact, leans in towards his subjects, and touches hands as he speaks. These clues may indicate that he is romantically interested in whomever he is talking to. In reality, that may be his way of showing interest in the conversation. It could almost be likened to respect.

Cultural differences may influence how we perceive certain behavior. For example, in the United States, we typically nod our head signifying, "Yes." However, in Greek cultures, a head nod means "No." In Portugal, individuals may tug their ears when something tastes delicious. Comical, yet true, Italians interpret this as a suggestive move with sexual undertones. Europeans kiss openly in public, whereas traditional Asian countries view this as inappropriate in public. The man mentioned earlier whose mannerisms may be suggestive probably grew up predominantly around women. His mother, no doubt, taught him how to show respect and interest to those to whom he is speaking. Although his actions came off as flirtatious, he was simply acting on a natural impulse. When analyzing others, it's key to remember that everyone comes from a different family that implemented different expectations for behavior. Some families may communicate through touching and warm embraces while another maintains a respectful distance. Before taking offense, consider how they grew up in conjunction with their personality. Perhaps they truly like you, and they are showing you in their own unique way.

Another key way to destroy perception from initial judgment is to get to know the person. Sure, someone may come off as rude, shy, aloof, or even angry. However, are they less deserving of having a social connection with you? Have they done anything concrete that prevents you from associating with them? The initial breaking of the ice may be challenging, but the results are worth it. When approaching someone who gives off negative body language, it's important to consider these tips if attempting to make a connection:

- Ask them about their interests.

- Discuss commonalities and attempt to make a connection.

- Ask them about their family. Do they have siblings? Is their family near or far?

- Share something special about yourself. This may open the door for further conversation.

- Simply ask them how their day is going.

There are a plethora of ice breakers that can be used to approach someone who may seem unapproachable. By doing so, you will learn that, although perception is key, understanding is what shapes relationships. You could be passing up on a purposeful friendship because of a misunderstanding. By taking the additional time to understand someone else, you will then understand their body language. You will learn what encompasses their inner being. This will help you to develop an open mind when building relationships.

CHAPTER 8

COMMON PATTERNS OF INTERPRETING BEHAVIOR – LEGS AND FEET

When engaging in a conversation, we typically don't pay attention to the movements of the lower body. Since our direct line of sight is from the chest up, we often miss the obvious signs of the legs and feet. Certain stances that occur within the legs can signify dominance, sexual attraction, and even anxiety. Let's consider a few common patterns to look for when attempting to analyze someone else.

Crossed Legs

Crossed legs could indicate defensiveness. Perhaps you are sitting in a meeting at work, and your colleague says something totally off-putting. You may find yourself slowly crossing your legs as a subliminal way of showing your disapproval. Defensiveness could be heightened when one hand is positioned on top of the crossed leg. This is almost like a taunting move, signaling combat.

Crossing the ankles or knees are signs of nervousness, anxiety, and fear. This stance is protective in nature, which indicates that someone is attempting to protect themselves from whatever source of fear they are encountering. It could also be a means to control actions during high adrenaline situations.

Pointing and Active Legs

If you are miserable at a party, likely your legs are pointed towards the door as you are ready to leave. Our legs inadvertently point to where our heart wants to go. This can be used to determine interest and attraction. The legs, even when covered, will almost always point in the direction they are interested in.

Legs that bounce continuously could mean two things: boredom and nervousness. When you witness a person continuously bouncing their legs up and down, they may be nervous about something. This bounce is like a protective blanket that distracts their mind from their jitters. In addition, when someone is growing restless and ready to go, they may move their legs rapidly. The bouncing or tapping of the legs can be likened to a compulsion carried out to make the irritation subside.

When both legs point in one direction, it could be a clear indicator of interest for the person. However, when one leg steps back, it could indicate that the person wants distance. They may be uncomfortable with the person, conversation, or situation at hand. This subtle movement could be their way of escaping something distressful.

Messages from the Thighs

The upper portions of the legs usually indicate sexual or suggestive invitations between men and women. In daily activities, men may sit with their thighs opened as a sign of dominance. This outward display of masculinity represents an "alpha male" mentality. With women, closed thighs are a polite sign of femininity. Many young girls are instructed to sit with their legs closed so as not to expose their private areas. This closed manner of sitting is graceful and emanates class. When opened, they express dominance and even a form of female rebellion. Since it is so common for girls to be taught to keep their legs closed, doing the opposite could indicate opposition to societal norms. In addition, it is also extremely flirtatious to sit with the thighs crossed and one sitting higher above the other. This could indicate interest.

The Feet

The feet work very closely with the legs to determine areas of interest. When the toes are pointed at a specific object or direction, this indicates where we want to go. This could be a subtle signal your body sends to your mind about certain situations. The feet are used to make a statement and could also be used as an accent to verbal cues. Stomping, imaginative kicking, or tapping are all means of gaining attention.

When toddlers throw tantrums, it's not only their flailing arms, crying eyes, and yelling demands that occur. Toddlers utilize their legs and feet to create loud noises to further emphasize their anger.

Much like moving the legs, bouncing the feet or excessive pacing are signs of anxiety. During moments of high adrenaline, the feet can be seen moving uncontrollably, almost like rabbit's feet. Signs of nervousness are also present when the feet are curled behind an object, perhaps the legs of a chair or a table. Since curving the body inward is a subtle sign of inner protection, the feet follow suit with this protective stance.

Professor Geoffrey Beattie of the University of Manchester reveals that subtle foot movements and positioning could reveal signs of personality traits. He explains, "The weird thing about feet is that most people know what they are doing with their facial expressions; they may or may not know what they are doing with their hands, but unless we specifically think about it, we know nothing about what we are doing with our feet." Through his studies, he found that individuals with rather arrogant or haughty personalities typically kept their feet still as they were always aware of the self; whereas, shy individuals frequently shuffled their feet when sitting. This gives us insight into the characteristics of a person. Typically, shy people indicate high levels of nervousness or anxiety during social occasions. This directly proves the notion that foot movement equals anxiety. The beauty behind interpreting subtle body movements is that you can always find a glimmer of proof to solidify the theory.

Feet are also directly related to laughter. When we are extremely tickled by something, our feet come slightly off the ground. We may even partner that laughter with a slap of the knee. Dr. Beattie mentioned that men and women subconsciously show their attraction by combining feet movement during laughter. This indicates that the woman is comfortable enough with you to make obvious movements. As far as men, he says, "With men, feet aren't so important. With men it's more head tilting. Women often tilt their heads, and it is often thought to be a feminine thing. But actually, it's men who play a slightly more submissive role."

When it comes to interpreting the signs of the legs and feet, direction and movement are the two primary components needed for translation. Although we typically fret from glancing at the bottom half of a person, simple movements could be a key indicator as to how a person is feeling. It's imperative to understand the beauty of intricate movements in order to fully understand the inner workings of another person.

CHAPTER 9

COMMON PATTERNS OF INTERPRETING BEHAVIOR - ARMS AND HANDS

A great deal of our emotions are expressed through our arms and hands. The warm embrace of a touch indicates love while a sharp slap translates to anger. Much of our productivity depends on the accuracy of our arms and hands when completing tasks. The movements of the arms and hands are quite obvious as they are used as a complement to verbal expression. Let's consider a few subliminal signals we receive from analyzing the hands and arms.

As our arms expand, we typically appear larger than our normal demeanor. This could be used as a descriptive means to explain how massive a person or object is, or this could be a subtle sign of instigating aggression or dominance. It also indicates spatial awareness. A person could expand the arms to give the subtle signal that they prefer space. It could be likened to "marking their territory." On the contrary, when the arms expand but curve towards the person, this is reminiscent of a hug. This embrace indicates safety or protection. Many mother figures are seen welcoming their children in this manner.

Since we primarily use our hands and arms to gesture, they are extremely descriptive tools that express our emotions. When the arms are raised, this is a sign of frustration and overwhelming doubt. We can almost envision an overwhelmed person clenching their hands over their ears or on top of the head as a means of protection.

The crossing of the arms is a true indicator of how a person is feeling. As previously mentioned, when the arms are crossed, this typically means anxiety, shyness, fear, or disbelief. We can picture a frustrated mother or father crossing their arms towards their child when they do something naughty. However, when the arms are tightly crossed with the hands either balled into fists or nestled in the armpits, this signals combat. This occurs when an individual has been taunted. Their anger is essentially holding their arms inward as a protective means. The hidden fists could signal the person holding themselves back from doing something they would regret.

Individuals who have been exposed to violence or who feel vulnerable may have a strong dislike for people speaking to them with their hands in their faces. Even a slight gesture could signal a fight or flight response. When the arms are thrusting forward, this is a scare tactic usually intended to create emphasis. We fight with our arms and hands, so the connection between the two is threatening.

When the arms are positioned behind the backs and out of sight of the person they are engaging with, this indicates hidden intent. The person may lack confidence, or they are attempting to hide their fear through fiddling with their hands behind their backs. This isn't necessarily a sign of a liar. Rather, the person may simply feel uncomfortable, or they are preventing themselves from saying something.

The elbows, when facing out, could be a silent cry for space. A person may want others to back away from them without having to actually verbally express their disposition. This can easily be observed through the actions of children. Toddlers, who cannot communicate verbally, will often extend their elbows in a sharp motion in order to indicate space. As adults, we do this subconsciously as a means of inner protection.

The hands are quite detailed in their means of communication. One move of the hand can indicate an invitation while another movement could ignite conflict. When the hands are crossed with the thumbs tucked under, this is a signal of peace. East Indian gurus can be seen holding their hands in this way to express giving, peaceful natures. They wish to extend this light to others through their physical movements. When the hands are placed in front of the belly button, with the fingers touching and open palms, this is a symbol of dignity. The person is trying to show their partner that they are confident, professional, and conscientious.

The hands are also key indicators of direction. We use our fingers to point towards areas of interest. When the hands are placed delicately on the knees with the palms down, this could indicate submission, especially when leaning towards the opposite person. Women usually engage in this stance while attempting to show interest in a flirtatious manner. Hand gestures can also indicate movement. When the palm is facing a person, this translates to dismissal and disapproval. The person is using their hands to physically block the other person from their sight.

When the hands are touching parts of the face, this could translate to brainstorming, boredom, or even decision making. When the palms are essentially holding the face and cheeks upward, this is a clear indicator of a person attempting to wake themselves up from a boring situation. It shows disinterest in the most obvious of ways. However, when the index finger is pointing towards certain areas of the face, a person could be deep in thought. The positioning of the fingers as well as the firmness of their grasp is telling.

Excessive shaking that permeates throughout the palms and into the fingers occurs during high stress situations. A person may be so nervous, their hands begin to shake uncontrollably. This also is a sign of intense hunger. The hands and fingers begin to grow unsteady, thus displaying the body's lack of food. Slight trembles can also occur when a person is being caught in a lie or confronted for a mistake. They may be so angry that the shakes are their way of expressing that anger.

We use our hands to describe the size and stature of certain things. Much like the arms, they are used to accentuate the gravity of a story, describe the weightiness of a subject, and even demonstrate movement. They are our primary way of gesturing, and they can add great excitement to a story or a conversation. When working together with the arms, the hands can be a great indicator of a person's confidence. Touching creates a sense of warmth and community that connects people together. When analyzed carefully, the movement of the hands and arms can tell us key clues about a person's disposition.

CHAPTER 10

HOW TO SPOT A LIE - KEY BEHAVIOR THAT INDICATES DECEPTION

Detecting deceit will give you the rare opportunity to choose your associates wisely without having to say a word. The body goes into an immense ball of anxiety when a person lies. The trained eye will be able to detect these small variances that occur. Although words may speak their version of the truth, the body never lies. Deceit is the act of covering up the way you truly feel through seeking control. Oftentimes, that control is executed in a sloppy manner, thus leading to dominant cues that signal deceit. Whether it's a large lie or a little white lie, the results of dishonesty come with a variety of consequences. Essentially, people lie as a subconscious form of protection. They are either hiding their negative behavior or protecting their reputations. Even when used to exaggerate a story, they may be attempting to protect the fact that their life is truly boring. They want others to find them enjoyable. Thus, various lies are told.

One organization divides deceit into four categories of explanation and uses:

Anxiety- seeking to hide the fact that they are nervous

Control- gestures or smiles that are forced or a grand attempt to stop the body from moving

Distraction- Frequent pausing or bodily actions in between answers is that person's attempt to distract you from their lie. By acting out these grand gestures, they believe they are making their stories believable.

Persuasion- Deceit may stem from wanting someone to carry out an action which will result in the liar's favor.

Joseph Tecce, a researcher at Boston College, exposed the six reasons why individuals lie in addition to their respective character traits:

1. Protective Lies: This protects the reputation of the liar or even the victim from undue harm. They seek to keep their social status by not revealing true behavior.

2. Heroic Liars: These individuals will lie in an attempt to uphold the greater good. For example, a popular episode of *Sex and the City* portrayed Carrie and her friend, Stanford, at a mixer. Stanford was interested in a handsome man across the room. He asked Carrie to go and find out if the man was gay or straight. She approached him and let him know of

Stanford's interest. The man looked at Stanford from across the room in utter repulsion. As Carrie went back to her hopeful friend, she told him that the handsome man was straight. She wanted to protect her friend's self-esteem by not revealing the truth.

3. Playful Liars: Playful liars accentuate their stories in order to provide a means of entertainment for listeners.

4. Ego Liars: Ego liars will cover mistakes in order to protect their reputations or status.

5. Gainful Liars: These are people who lie for personal gain.

6. Malicious Liars: These are the individuals who are out to seek revenge and harm others due to psychological challenges.

Many individuals are so crafty at lying; they have mastered the art of concealing their body movements. Sociopaths and psychopaths alike are so deranged; they feel no emotional connection to the lies. It is quite difficult to detect their inaccuracies because they are so connected to the lies. They may even begin to believe the lies. When considering the deceit of mentally stable individuals, however, there may be concrete reasons behind their excessive lying. Let's consider a few signs of a deceitful person and consider their traits.

The head can offer a slight indication of a person beginning to lie. When being asked a question, a liar tends to quickly move their head prior to responding. Interestingly, the face holds many of the truest signs of deception. We express honest emotions through the theory of timing. Researchers have found that, naturally, we hold our expressions between one and four seconds. When a person is lying or faking an emotion, the expression is usually held for a longer period of time. In addition, their symmetrical alignment can play a huge role in detecting insincerity. To tell if a person is being honest, notice the purest emotions are evenly distributed throughout the face. However, a liar will typically express their emotions on one side dominantly. Our speech and body movements should complement each other. So if a person is telling you how beautiful you look while frowning and crossing their arms, it is safe to conclude that they aren't genuine.

Excessive body movements are often associated with nervousness. Naturally, though, the body engages in slight movements even without the presence of anxiety. However, Dr. Leanne Brinke, professor of the Haas School of Business, indicates that a person who remains as still as a statue should be further examined. She says, "You should be just as wary of those who do not move at all as this may be related to the human 'fight or flight' instinct, specifically the option to 'fight.' As a result of this instinct, the body tenses itself in preparation for potential confrontation." Have you ever noticed that when catching someone in a lie, their body tends to freeze almost like a deer caught in headlights? Essentially, they are shocked that their behavior has been caught. At that moment, they have lost all control, and they feel exposed. In order to gain some form of control, they clench their body.

It is also key to notice where their hands go when being confronted. Do they cover their mouths? Throats? Chests? By providing this subtle distraction, they are protecting themselves from the truth. They have no intention of telling the truth, so they are, in effect, covering areas of the body that assist with communication. In addition, verbal cues also point towards deception. Excessive repeating, stuttering, and clearing of the throat are key signs of nervousness. They are desperately trying to buy time to respond.

Traditionally, the eyes have been closely associated with deceit. Previously, we spoke about the connection between dilation and interest. When we see something we love or are attracted to, our eyes dilate. When in a relationship, a key indicator of a loss of interest rests in the pupils. When you ask your mate if your outfit looks great, they may say it looks awesome, but the pupils tell the truth. Excessive darting of the eyes or an avoidance of eye contact signifies some level of deceit. The person may be attempting to put on the demeanor of aggression, but they refuse to look at another's eyes. Are they truly as tough as they say they are? Interestingly, the right side of the brain controls auditory processing, big picture ideas, and decision making. When a person darts their eyes downward and towards the right, they are attempting to envision something, perhaps visiting a place they have never been. They may look down and to the right when thinking about what it's like to live there. When someone is lying, notice how they may repeat this same motion. Interestingly, they are attempting to envision something that didn't occur rather than recall a memory.

The body is also a clear indicator of deceit. You may notice the person's breathing patterns significantly speed up. Their chest could move faster, and their breathing becomes louder. Their shoulders and elbows are stiffly raised. This movement represents being caught, as seen depicted in cartoons. The robber may inadvertently stop in their tracks with their shoulders raised. They are trying to protect themselves by growing defensive. Psychics and spiritual healers utilize exposed palms to reveal truth. Although controversial, many readers analyze the open palms to detect repressed emotions, predict future occurrences, and decode personality. When a person is lying, those palms of truth are suddenly closed and facing away from the subject. It's a subconscious way of not wanting to reveal their truth.

Although detecting liars is an essential tool to have, simply noticing a liar isn't productive. Effective communication in conjunction with understanding can help to reveal lies and reach solutions.

CHAPTER 11

HOW TO SPOT ROMANTIC INTEREST - BODY LANGUAGE CUES THAT SIGNAL ATTRACTION

Being able to detect if a person is truly into you can save a lot of time and heartache when dating. There are specific body movements that are unique to men and women that display attraction. Sure, words are powerful, but actions are groundbreaking. This form of body language is the most sensual in nature and inviting. Many of the common depictions on cartoons and illustrations are quite accurate when it comes to flirting. Women have a unique set of body language cues that are attractive to men. It complements their feminine role and can be used as a form of luring the man in. Men demonstrate a similar display of body cues that align with their masculinity. Oftentimes, the cues are so strong, they release certain hormones related to sexual attraction. The act of engaging in sexual pleasure is body language at its height.

Since words are not commonly used as a sexual act, intercourse is the purest form of visually displaying that attraction. However, the journey from first date to the bedroom is filled with subtle clues that could alter the destination. Let's consider the primary difference between men and women when it comes to displaying attraction.

Women

When a woman finds a male attractive, she may begin by locking eyes with him. She could give a subtle gaze and then look away. If this continues, the woman essentially wants the man to chase her. Simple touches to the body and even her curling her hair with fingers are used to flirt. This brings attention to the feminine qualities of a woman that may be attractive to the man. When a woman raises her eyebrows when talking with a man, they are signaling attraction. She may find the man to be physically handsome or admirable. Or she may be so caught up in what he is saying that it moves her to agree. The lips also indicate attraction especially in the biting, licking, or caressing them. When a woman looks intently at a man's lips and then makes direct eye contact, this is a subconscious invitation to kiss.

As mentioned previously, women tend to lean in toward their dates to show attraction. When her legs are crossed inward, facing her date, it's a suggestive pose that indicates sexual interest. This is heightened when the genitals are exposed and involve a light caress. Women may also arch their backs to further elongate their spines.

The curvature of their spine is a feminine quality that is attractive to the man. Slight exposure of the breast is a sign of intense flirtation. She is drawing the man into her womanhood to express interest.

Women may also "bat" their eyes up and down rapidly as a sign of flirtation. This brings attention to the lashes which, when elongated, are physically pleasing to the man. She may pair this with a slight giggle to signal attraction.

Oftentimes, women tend to "mirror" the movements of men. This signifies submission as the woman is showing respect for the position of the man. Inadvertently, she is following the lead of her date. Many sensual dances rely on the man leading and the woman following. Women subconsciously perform these acts as a means to show respect for the men's masculinity.

Men

When a man moves his head slightly, raises his brows, and allows his nostrils to flare, he is indicating attraction. When paired with a smile, the level of attraction is heightened. Initially, a man will avoid making direct eye contact as he may be nervous or unaware of the woman's attraction level. In addition, men speak with their chest. If the chest is pointing towards the woman, he is giving her his full attention. If his chest is pointing elsewhere, he secretly wants to escape the situation.

Men want to appear dominant, masculine, and strong to perspective dates. They may stand with their feet wide and their hands on their hips in order to appear sturdy. If his hands are gracing his waist line, he essentially wants the woman to look near his genitals. This is a silent invitation to a possible sexual encounter. Men tend to show their attraction through their hands. Slight touches to the back, thigh, and arm indicates sexual attraction. However, a pat on the shoulder could be read as platonic.

There are universal signs of attraction carried out by both men and women. Smiling and a willingness to laugh without apprehension are valuable signs. Spatial awareness is a key indicator to revealing intent. When two people are attracted to each other, they tend to stand close. Their shoulders are raised and positioned inwardly which indicates interest. Even the positioning of the toes symbolizes attraction. As mentioned, the toes point to where they want to go. When the toes are facing each other, sometimes called "pigeon toed," they are subtle signs of flirting. The man or woman wants to appear cute and coy. This vulnerable position subconsciously boosts sexual attraction. The palms traditionally reveal truth. When a man or a woman is interested, their palms may rest in an exposed position. It promotes openness which indicates that the two would like to get to know each other.

The laws of attraction are traditional as they signify small psychological changes that are quite universal. When a person speaks their intent with body language cues to follow, you can guarantee their validity. By understanding these simple cues, you will be better equipped to make accurate perceptions about the intent of others.

CHAPTER 12

HOW TO SPOT INSECURITY - SMALL SIGNS THAT SHOW A LACK OF CONFIDENCE

When people lack confidence, they display those characteristics boldly. Their posture and demeanor speak volumes so loud; others immediately respond. Unfortunately, these body positions prevent individuals from being treated with respect. They are more susceptible to being taken advantage of, passed up for opportunities, and even disrespected. Why is this the case?

Our brain perceives certain body movements as being weak. Previously, we discussed different body movements that signal submission. While having a submissive personality is generally accepted as being mild, it doesn't equate a lack of confidence. Moreover, the body cues being demonstrated are similar in nature but intricately different. One of the primary indicators of a person lacking self-confidence is engaging in extremes. This can be found when individuals attempt to become "larger than life" by outward displays of dominance. Their initial appearance may seem intimidating, but their core is weak. They exude this fake confidence as a mask to cover up their inner conflict. Obnoxious, loud, domineering, and dismissive gestures are used to compensate for something they are lacking. Whether it's physical beauty, intelligence, or inner insecurities, your untrained eye may view them with admiration, even succumbing to their ploys. Once you are trained, it is quite obvious for you to see through their excessive demeanor.

Posture

A person's posture says a lot about their inward confidence. A tall, relaxed back indicates true confidence. There is nothing forced or excessively pronounced. When a person seems to loom over others with a widened stance, they are seeking authority. They may feel insecure about their current lot in life, so they attempt to make others feel small physically. In addition, slouched shoulders, a downturned chin, and legs close together are obvious signs of insecurity. The way a person positions himself in a chair also speaks volumes. If they are slouched, with arms tightly crossed, they are attempting to protect themselves. They may suffer from social anxiety and seek to disappear.

Eye Contact

As previously mentioned, direct eye contact reveals confidence. When a person avoids making eye contact with someone by looking away or downward, they are secretly wishing to escape. They are fearful of what the other person is thinking, so they retreat to a safe space. You can always tell when someone is forcing eye contact as they blink less frequently in an attempt to control the direction of their eyes. In summation, their gaze isn't natural. It appears forced and likely strange.

Touching the Self

In an attempt to distract themselves from the current situation, insecure people will often fiddle with their teeth, touch their heads, or rub areas of their bodies. This is not an inviting or suggestive means to seduce. Rather, it's a coping mechanism used to calm the body and mind. This is why nail biting is often associated with being nervous.

When individuals constantly fiddle with their clothing or readjust certain aspects of their appearance, they may feel insecure about their outward appearance. They may feel the need to fix themselves in order to fit the expectations of those around them. Oftentimes, people who try out new looks may constantly mess with their clothing because they are not accustomed to the style.

Excessive Movements

Leg, arm, and hand movements indicate nervousness or anxiety. When a person fidgets with different sections of the body, this is another sign of self-soothing. They are nervous about the conversation or even the environment they are in. You may notice that public speakers tend to fiddle with their ring or wrists when speaking about a challenging topic. In addition, placing your hands in your pockets, thus hiding them from the public, is a sign of apprehension. You are sending the message of fear as you are attempting to conceal something.

As mentioned, the reverse is true for individuals who are immensely insecure. They attempt to overcompensate for what they are lacking by relying on superiority. Alfred Adler was a groundbreaking psychologist who studied human behavior. He thoroughly researched what he named the inferiority complex which addresses exaggerated behaviors as a means to gain respect. Adler said people who feel inferior go about their days overcompensating through what he called "striving for superiority." According to the article, "The only way these inwardly uncertain people can feel happy is by making others decidedly unhappy." These individuals may use excessive physical displays of anger as a means to gain control and ignite fear.

The slamming of doors, banging on desks, and even hanging up the phone with force are classic signals. When engaging in conversation, they rarely make eye contact perhaps busying themselves with other tasks. This outright dismissiveness is their way of showing others how important they think they are. On the inside, they may be recovering from past experiences of not being listened to. They may make others feel inferior as a means to seek revenge.

Another sign of insecurity is excessive laughing. As a means to fill the gap of conversation, a person may nervously laugh excessively. They are drastically uncomfortable and are at a loss for words. They may feel that laughing gives them the opportunity to make a fake connection. This could be accompanied by uncomfortable sweating or blushing. The body is physically revealing signs of embarrassment which increases our body temperature. Sweat may begin to lightly appear. The person may even begin to feel increasingly self-conscious about their sweat as well.

In this technology-filled world, cell phones are like extensions of the body. If a person constantly fiddles with their phone during social outings, they are probably suffering from extreme discomfort. They are attempting to calm their nerves through a cell phone screen. They may find scrolling through their social media as a form of comfort as it distracts them from actually engaging in a conversation.

Detecting insecurity isn't meant to give you power over vulnerable individuals. Rather, it is an inward ability to adjust your reactions to their behavior. If you encounter someone who is seeking to overcompensate by making others feel bad, you can detect that and handle them accordingly. You can see past their demeanor and ignore their "threats." When encountering a traditionally insecure person, you will know how to handle them with care. This knowledge will boost your ability to establish successful relationships and even boost social morale.

CONCLUSION

The body is a fascinating group of systems that work coherently to expose our innermost emotions. From a simple glimpse of the eyes all the way down to the positioning of the toes, the body is honest. Mastering the art of analyzing others begins with a comprehensive understanding of yourself. Even different inflections of the voice can change a sentence in its entirety. In addition, the art of touch can mean the difference between attraction and repulsion. Learning how to analyze others assists with social connection and your ability to understand what others are truly saying. The beauty behind the human connection is that there are universal mannerisms that give off social cues open for interpretation. A simple shrug of the brows paired with a crossing of the arms signals a sign of discontent. A slight lean inward can give you the signal that your date is legitimately into you! These subtle cues are intricate in nature, but the magnitude is revolutionary. By mastering these techniques, you will have this unwavering gift that is easily applicable to your everyday life. You will be able to seek the truth and defend yourself against possible threats. One of the key secrets to mastering the art of analyzing others is keying in on your observation skills. The entire body works in conjunction with the brain to send and expel certain messages that define emotions, often leading to subconscious visual cues that may give away the true thoughts and feelings of a given individual without their even realizing what they are doing. Inside, you will find dozens of different ways to pick up on those cues for fun and profit. By being observant and truly reading the behaviors of others, you will be able to emphasize this gift to meet your needs. We encourage you to implement these practices into your daily life to further analyze yourself and truly be able to read others.

The next step is to practice these tips throughout your daily life! By doing so, you will gain a better understanding of yourself and human behavior as a whole.

Finally, if you found this book useful in any way, a review on Amazon is always appreciated!

Made in the USA
Lexington, KY
05 November 2018